BECOS

BECOS

POEMS BY

BILL KNOTT

RANDOM HOUSE NEW YORK

Earlier versions of a few of these poems appeared in *Antaeus, Ironwood*
and *The Paris Review*.

"The Closet" originally appeared in *Ironwood*. Other
selections appeared in the following publications:
Antaeus, Cincinnati Poetry Review, The Missouri Review,
and *The Paris Review*.

Library of Congress Cataloging in Publication Data

Knott, Bill, 1940-
Becos: poems.

I. Title.
PS3561.N65B4   1983   811'.54   82-16712
ISBN 0-394-52924-3

Manufactured in the United States of America

2   4   6   8   9   7   5   3

First Edition

TO JEAN KILBOURNE

According to a story in Herodotus,
becos (Phrygian for "bread") was the
first word spoken by the human race . . .

Thanks to the following folks: Naomi Lazard, Paul Carroll, John Schultz, James Randall, C. K. Williams, Gary Pacernick, Charles Simic, Russell Banks, Robert Bly, Tom Lux, Grace Shulman, Tess Gallagher, William Matthews, Jim Heynen, George Starbuck, Larry Levis, Marsha Southwick, Paul Hoover, Maxine Chernoff, Marjorie Hunt, Ellen Bryant Voigt, Heather MacHugh, Mary Karr, Lindsay Knowlton, Keith Hollaman, Rochelle Nameroff, and The MacDowell Colony, The Millay Colony for the Arts, The Centrum Arts Center, David Wilk for my N.E.A., and my students at Columbia College, Thomas Jefferson College, Wright State University, and Emerson College. Don't forget Bill Zavatsky.

And—special thanks to Ginny MacKenzie, whose friendship and lendable ears have meant everything, and without whose kindness and editorial wisdom these poems would not be.

CONTENTS

❧ ❧ ❧ ❧ ❧

I

THE PAST
AS PEDAGOGUE

GENERIC: AFTER READING
PLATH AND SEXTON

Eyelashes did their job:
they lengthened the afternoon,
like a dress hem.

Then that night the hem began to rise, in stages
revealing
scenes from my shameful life.

—Those calves
up which the hem reproachfully rasped,
catching,
lingering over whatever scene
(the higher the younger) arose
on those calves
knees, thighs, those
woman segments

or were they mine—
I hid my eyes.
I wouldn't attend to
the walls either

endless walls, slowly
basted
with suicide.

The eyelashes did their job.
But I, who could neither sew
nor cook groped and groped those long legs
stubborn, afraid to look.

MORE GUILT

Even now, when I patrol my thoughts of you
I still remember
to put a danger behind each dark bush

Like death's monogram
on a christmas gift, each omen
suspicious-snapped twig bears your stamp
No longer blatantly disguised as pain. —Though

pain passes for sunlight at some depths

(Those depths:
there's where I guess one can see even more clear
those cruelly-elegant tablehoppers so affable
Each seated alone
atop a Himalaya

their black silks
Helicopters whisk them a cocktail
at night, the stars shine like gnawed thimbles)

Go away! I have no child-brides in eternity—
Even now I must flash the unhex sign, fearfully
repeat this ward-off charm:
I have no child-brides in eternity,
I have no . . . etc.

MY FAULT

Six AM the
Clockhands
Clothespins
Of nakedness

Is it turn for your shadow to be
The sun's birthmark or mine
We lie in the ruins the pertains
Of all we sought to evade by touch, avoid by sight

Now we argue over which criteria
Gravity uses to select its victims
Why weigh the impact of our caresses upon
This bed till they fade, svelte
As a thumbsdown swan?

Only the sun rises at random, at mootpoint we lie
The rain wearing black armbands may pass,
I dab my smile at the mournersby
I dab my heart at you.
As for the blame, I'll take it:

I was naked there, where we were.
I was naked,
But my clothes were stuck in my throat, thereby
Rendering my nakedness ineffectual (or, perhaps, spurious)?

I would of whispered something darling
But there was this darn zipper
Right up against my voicebox

🐝 5

THE CONSOLATIONS OF SOCIOBIOLOGY

Those scars rooted me. Stigmata stalagmite
I sat at a drive-in and watched the stars
Through a straw while the coke in my lap went
Waterier and waterier. For days on end or

Nights no end I crawled on all fours or in
My case no fours to worship you: Amoeba Behemoth.
—Then you explained your DNA calls for
Meaner genes than mine and since you are merely

So to speak its external expression etcet
Ergo among your lovers I'll never be. . .
Ah that movie was so faraway the stars melting

Made my thighs icy. I see: it's not you
Who is not requiting me, it's something in you
Over which you have no say says no to me.

LESSON

Our love has chosen its appropriate gesture
Which when viewed in the midst of all the gestures
It didn't choose seems almost insignificant.

The gesture our love has chosen is appropriate
We both agree not that we have any choice but
Amidst all those others does seem insignificant.

Is it incumbent on us thus to therefore obliterate
All of the gestures except this insignificant one
Chosen by our love for its own no doubt reasons.

It is up to us to obliterate all other gestures
Though they cluster round thick as presentations
Of war and sacrifice in a gradeschool classroom.

Use of our love's chosen gesture for the obliteration
Of all those foreign gestures is forbidden however
We must find something else to erase them with.

Our love has chosen its appropriate gesture
Which when viewed in the absence of all other gestures
Seems to spell the opposite of insignificant.

FOR LACK OF YOU

I examine the sun's diagrams
for your tan. The ground's plans for your walk.
Sky's project-papers on how, where
to utilize your breaths. All these schemata,
endless as my tracings of your faraway
face. Poring over them in a solarium
observatory devoted to the study
of you. New proposals, blueprints
flood in each moment: slowly reading, hoping, finally
I grow feeble-eyed—. The fineprint for
your lashes, the arms' down, fades. Now
you're crude, a block, an abstract
obstruction or any old construction of
skylines, vague unhouseholds. The plumbing
venues, vent of window or door
vanished, even the light itself a blur—
at last comes total blindness:
touch-awkward I feel like an ogre, a clumsy giant
tripping over some ruins,
rubble of the town he's just smashed.
Tower-cursing as I bang my knee. Or no:
I'm tiny. I can see again! I see the giant walk off
favoring his one leg. . .favoring
my one you, I kick through
the strewn clutter, I get down on my knees
and start to scour around; one model, just one
to copy from, to begin again. That's
all I need, lacking you.

THE PERMISSION

On each shoulder
               I bear
a jar
    with each
its angel
       in
           formaldehyde
I wish to preserve my loves
                  You
say No
      let them go fly way
                away
and when
        they come back and
                  if then
then you
        may kiss me on
each shoulder gone wing.

EXTINCTIONS, SCHEDULE OF

Each time the words physic or psychic appeared
we had to stop think now which means which.
This dyslexia extended, soon

we couldn't make out who loved who when, where,
or the prospects. Sometimes, it's so hard to know,
and what you take for eagerness is just jumpcuts.

But how systematize—name-down everything down
to its component night- and light-crawlers, when
everyone longs to remain unplaceable, a pastel brick.

Like lounging pilgrims who break off car aerials,
we wrote WASH ME in the dust
of a remnant grave in an old mutants'-cemetery.

Vandals or angels? Non sequitur. Original sin and shinola?
We traced out all archaic infantile guilts,
killing them with a lullaby alibi.

Some of us toptenned with exposes on over-the-shoulderites,
    nth-inchers, cross-offs.
Others simply exhibited ourselves, looking devious and
    assaulted
like a mugshot of a child.

Ancestor-silencing is difficult when you you're the one
who forgot to patent the dodo.
Then on to the next name on the list, pen pointing—

Many times we sped to the bus-station and waved
to the ticket-seller, the newsie, the floor-sweeper,
but, they didn't ever leave.

Neither did the cold-drink machine.
Our farewells lacked the plausibility of our departures.
We went on squeezing all the soft, wishy places in our flesh,

out gushed mail, letters, postcards, so-so ultimata.
We were writing out of a faith whose idols had crumbled.
Smattered features we could no longer. . .uh, read.

MITTS AND GLOVES

FOR TOM LUX

The catcher holds a kangaroo fetus in his,
the firstbaseman's grips a portable hairblower,

but everyone else just stares into theirs
punching a fist into it, stumped

trying to come up with a proper occupant—
The pitcher for example thinks a good stout padlock would go

right in there, but the leftfielder,
perhaps influenced by his environment,

opts for a beercan. The shortstop
informative about the ratio of power to size,

says "Transistor. You know, radio." The
secondbaseman however he just stands and

grins and flapjacks his from hand to hand and back again,
secondbase dopey as always. Alas

cries the thirdbaseman, this void
of vacancy, pure-space beyond our defiant emptiness,—

abyss, haunted by the kiss of balls
we have not missed! oh absence

delice. . .The rightfielder looks dis-
gusted at this, he just snorts, hawks, spits

into his and croaks Hey look: heck,
my chaw of tobac fits it perfeck.

The team goes mum, cowhided by
the rectitude of his position, the logic.

Only the centerfielder, who was going back
while this discussion was going on,

putting jets on his cleats to catch the proverbial
long one,

does he perhaps have a suggestion. . .?
As for the ball, off in mid air it dreamily

scratches its stitches and wonders
what it will look like tomorrow when it wakes up

and the doctor removes its bandages—

CODA
Mitts are whitecollar; professionals;—
designed for firstbase, homeplate, unique, elite,—

and therefore moral. The glove on the
other hand is human and can be worn

interchangeably by
all players; 's dirty, low-down, dumb. I'm

forced to admire the mitt but
free (in theory) to love gloves.

THE VIGILANCES OF EVENING

1.

The sun goes down, slush
on radar-screens— My screens go down
also, at this hour, memories ping up, take shape;
mind clings to them, gently,
as icicles hang from a cobweb so it won't rip;
I'm torn in two
to remember that rubble-down-on farmhouse
of my youth,
—its scrub-brick cellar,
which should more or rough take a thrift-year's canning,
wall to wall cloth by now. The spider
a meld-clone of Dior and Dali, flings
a grid on which things die, all things torn
from those false skies of the past; shot-down jets
of Korea, sentimentalized sunsets
the cowboy merged his horse-hips with: against that mesh
of movie-screen mush
I see my defenses blip-out blank, burning,
a stealthless bomber
disseminates me then skids to rest in butterfly-nets, the
TV's zombie-zoom-lens. . .system is go. I read you. And
John Wayne in his cockpit and
me in my deathwatch
are part of this disinformation: under the CIA's shredder I
cross-thread and -weave these paperstrips into
what I'll call
(I remember out in Michigan in the country
they called what farmers did fieldwork)
an afield-work. . . .

The sun—but my metaphor's wrong: radar don't skein
or skim
non-earthly things. My lifewatch is on me then,
not them.

2.
Fizzle vigil. . .fiddle giggle. There's no escape. The day
flutters, it fades, faint as the wink
of an invalid flirting. . .

Someone comes, someone touches me, someone
as if they were examining my skin, searching
for the pore with EXIT over it.

THE CLOSET

(. . .after my Mother's death)

Not long enough after the hospital happened
I find her closet lying empty and stop my play
And go in and crane up at three blackwire hangers
Which quiver, airy, released. They appear to enjoy

Their new distance, cognizance born of the absence
Of anything else. The closet has been cleaned out
Full-flush as surgeries where the hangers could be
Amiable scalpels though they just as well would be

Themselves, in basements, glovelessly scraping uteri
But, here, pure, transfigured heavenward, they're
Birds, whose wingspans expand by excluding me. Their
Range is enlarged by loss. They'd leave buzzards

Measly as moths: and the hatshelf is even higher! —
As the sky over a prairie, an undotted desert where
Nothing can swoop sudden, crumple in secret. I've fled
At ambush, tag, age: six, must I face this, can

I have my hide-and-seek hole back now please, the
Clothes, the thicket of shoes, where is it? Only
The hangers are at home here. Come heir to this
Rare element, fluent, their skeletal grace sings

Of the ease with which they let go the dress, slip,
Housecoat or blouse, so absolvingly. Free, they fly
Trim, triangular, augurs leapt ahead from some geometric
God who soars stripped (of flesh, it is said): catnip

To a brat placated by model airplane kits kids
My size lack motorskills for so I wind up glue-scabbed,
Pawing glaze skins, second fingernails fun to peer in as
Frost-i-glass doors. . .But the closet has no windows,

Opaque or sheer: I must shut my eyes, shrink within
To peep into this wall. Soliciting sleep I'll dream
Mother spilled and cold, unpillowed, the operating-
Table cracked to goad delivery: its stirrups slack,

Its forceps closed—by it I'll see mobs of obstetrical
Personnel kneel proud, congratulatory, cooing
And oohing and hold the dead infant up to the dead
Woman's face as if for approval, the prompted

Beholding, tears, a zoomshot kiss. White-masked
Doctors and nurses patting each other on the back,
Which is how in the Old West a hangman, if
He was good, could gauge the heft of his intended. . .

Awake, the hangers are sharper, knife-'n'-slice, I jump
Gropelessly to catch them to twist them clear,
Mis-shape them whole, sail them across the small air
Space of the closet. I shall find room enough here

By excluding myself; by excluding myself, I'll grow.

II

THE INTERIOR
MONOCLE

POET

FOR LOUISE GLUCK

Our eyes unlash slowly one
by one at last bald lids rise

What for

Mimicry
re
the poet's eye
looking inwards sees
minus its lashes' soft-pleaded intercedence
too pupilly cool cruel
as muttered justice

I call my goodbyes home in the
dusk

READER

Before going to the palmreader
I waxed my palms. . .opaque wax. . .so
the irrevocable lines and configurations that told my fate
were merely reflections of the reader's eyes,
eyelashes, retinal imperfections which time
will perhaps deepen glaucoma-wards. . .I was
about to p.s. these poems also. What do you see,
O Sibyl?

PER REQUEST

when we're always alone
and when we're never alone
which one
answers the phone

all that separates us
is the finishline
face in a race
with its own cheek bones

this toe to toe battle
with one's shadow
to gain possession
of a narrow choking ledge

the times
the time has come
I cower beneath my resurrections

OCTOBER

Time to pare down, pull in, simplify;
—I'll buy a dark coat, move my lips when I read
the bestseller-lists.

THE ENEMY

Like everyone I demand to be
Defended unto the death of
All who defend me, all the
World's people I command to
Roundabout me shield me, to
Fight off the enemy. The
Theory is if they all stand
Banded together and wall me
Safe, there's no one left to
Be the enemy. Unless I of
Course start attack, snap-
Ping and shattering my hands
On your invincible backs.

FBI KILLS MARTIN LUTHER KING

When this calendar has
undressed will I know, I mean
be able to recognize,
its most naked day—

but to see what is
in what was mistakes time
for its effect—I study
my hand, how
the palm hides in it, slyly,
or like a sullen puddle
refusing reflections—

and my 2-scoops-please blouse—
a passerby's
meander-fall hair—
though the sky's blue is through-outed
with spots of balm, do

they all
praise null but you,
null but them?

AT THE MUSEUM THIS WEEK

POLAND THROUGH THE CENTURIES a touring
Exhibition of maps drawn
By German and Russian cartographers reveals
There never was a Poland.

PENNY WISE

well alright
I grant you
he was a fascist
ahem antisemitism the
er war and all
I'm not defending them
but at least
you've got to admit
at least he
made the quatrains run on time

THE OLDEST STORY

As I grow older, can I grow better
learn more, love more, become a sage, get rich—
is improvement still possible
at this late stage of my life, as
for example it's possible to improve the phrase
'It is assuredly summer'
—if one works long and hard enough—to:
'It is assuredly autumn'
—and, with sweat coffeebreaks time redoubled
efforts, even this phrase can probably be. . .
     er, improved upon.

Imagine a Neandertal worrying about this topic!
Imagine the first one
to first leave the wise mountain,
the dreamers' caves, who decided
to go set up life below:
the one who came, naming what she led us into.

There is a valley is the oldest story.

(FACE) (AUTUMN) (EN FACE)

FOR NANCY SHERMAN LEWIS

I lay your face along my palm and make
To trace its shape there in profile
Then I see the lifeline heartline break
Overlengthened by one leaf's fall

The plow it rests on a horror now
In the distance an ogre pulls in vain
To open a nailed-shut window
Whose reverberency is thunder rain

Begins its rheumatization of
The world we shared so spare-much of that
This sans season's hands' veins portray our love

The no two alike are kissing yet
I lie down alone not knowing a tongue
Can taste every flavor but its own

OBSOLESCENT

Bending over like this to get my hands empty
Rummaging through the white trashcans out back
Of the Patent Office I find a kind of peace
Here in this warm-lit alley where no one comes.

Even the rats too they know that nothing new
Is going to get pitched out now—no formula,
Not one blueprint will ever be found in these
Bright bins whose futures are huge, pristine.

Old alleymouth grabbags my attention at times
I see the world flash by out there, glow-glow as
The floors of decontamination chambers—

I go back to my dull, boring search, foraging
For the feel it gives me of the thing which has
Invented me: that void whose sole idea I was.

ASSORTED SHORT POEMS

Wise Sayings

Sitting under a tree in the forest
or under a chair in the house
wise sayings may be misheard
or worse pass by unheard
through all these leaves and legs.

                *   *   *

Shame

In the whole universe I alone
Was unable to soften the impact,
Cushion the recoil of the M-16
Upon the M-17's shoulder.

                *   *   *

Prisoner

Some raw name scrapes and saws at my breath-hatch. . .
This voice wanted always only to soothe, not grate.
And its last noise, that rasp, that deathrale scratch?
—A file, smuggled in to an empty jail cell, too late.

THE SIGNS OF
THE STOPSIGN

Howsoever longer than life the entity they
proceed from is they are here termed too late or
to micro it, never. Names or signs it seems must

be functional or cease—scars too—until,
gentled genderless, they interrupt my babytalk
with teethingring-razors. . .then I woke up:

When, I asked an approaching closeup, do
I arrive? Gazes as found as mine in yours are
are sure to be lost amongst this sun dubbing

its gold into all tongues beneath stoplights that
change to go and ergo are not true, not whole?
Yet no sun holds us gunpoint as this, no sky:

in the hurt shirt of my breath worn
by no one I stand unbabbling another theory
(amnesiacs are laconic by necessity, not choice),—

to wit it's common data that 2 strangers are
sufficient for infinity's quorum, as long
as they never meet or is that lovers? Those

parallels called you and I prolong themselves past us
till at last we're wavelengthed through a room whose
wallpaper will eventually lapse back to

civilization in 2 or 3 hundred lousy rotten years,
we hope. For ever the speaklouders we hear now how
a spacesuit filled with dried feathers enters heaven

(pure alp up which the gaze drowns all hands lost)
to save us (our face chewed by drool of last dosages),
to zap the commies (in Sahara's waitingroom

the authentic and the false Sphinx continue
to ostentatiously ignore each other):—yet
persistent reconnaissance scanbacks show no one act-

ually evacuating his body despite these lethal warnings,
these vital-signs. . .And so the minus condition
of my nerves tonight alarms and the slow race

of my heart to repeat that somewhere
on the stopwatch is a time no sprinter
shall ever reach: can I believe them;—how can they

be mass enough medias for me to agree
to follow their old course? War, famine, morals
that have lost their fables: the signs

of the stopsign are everywhere. You my heart,
my head through which untold photographs zip.
I lie on a bed covered with stolen contact-lenses.

III

HOT GATES
AND TORRID
ENTRANCES

THE PANTHER

I didn't get his name the music of the dancehall
Was point to the noise and names of those people
In whose apartment we mostly ended up: I do recall
That, before squiring me through a bed or two, he
Kicked his dress across the room, aiming, I think,
At someone who stepped smirking back: perhaps a friend.

And the following morning, groping groggily
Toward the elevators something dragged, I looked down,
There it was, snarled round my shoe. Immediately
I stood reminded of a scene I can't for life say why:
A dancer, who has overslept, rushes by rote to dress
And ready a face all in a style obviously posthaste—

Clear to the ground floor I grinned at the inspection
Plaque and thought: I want her like that, that panicked.
—Unprepared as the rest of us went, when, virgin-awkward,
Each time we found ourselves under and in a fumble
For the unnatural rigor of alarm-clocks, or those
Damned thumb-blind button-holes, . . .—Is it, do I fear

Her second-knowledge gained from years of training,
—How that slow-gathered grace-of-artifice still
Outstrips us and is what will remain beyond our dumbshow
Pleasures, japes, these small oblivionings of each other in
The name of freeing ourself, well, me, really? —
And now her nine o'clock pupils attack their barre.

(SUN, SEA, RAIN) (RAIN SEASON) (PORT TOWNSEND, WASHINGTON)

FOR TESS GALLAGHER

—Each pine's sun-endowed
shadow follows April's down-
ward flights and where a crow's
muddy footprints show it sits
an initiating circle
on the ground and round
the wet grass, ring of council
I can be one in if I kneel,
remove my shoes and kneel, passing
some ancient peacepipe filled
with rain to my right
or are you supposed to go left—?
Once again, and always,
for not knowing the rules
OK, I get expelled—
fool. Or as James Tate
once called me in a poem, paralytic,
cripple. . .it's true: I sit
praying to join in, the
spiral prance, skip-heel hop
of your raindance, sun! but—
But what? Stamping
a cigaret out on an ant I kick at
my mildewed metaphor's
whatchama crutches,
wobbly props of pinless hopes:
I groan up, and walk, ouch,
soft-putty self-pity patched,
cussing the fact that
I no longer have the faith
I was born with; I await

the faith I will die with; and
meanwhile
the faith I live with, that
custodying lipserver, sticks
me near any old name-niche,
teeters me on
every pedestal of mislabeled
personae. . .so I watch
these madrona branches with a feel
for their similar swift elevations
downfalls—shifted by
(in descendent order,
and frequency:)
rainstorm, rain, and me.
I hear their leaf-whish as
an audio analogue of mist, which
is sister-common also, enhanceful,
to this place—

(Not an all at once thing, mist:
it curls into the world, pearl
being peeled)
                        —seemingly other parings litter
the ocean water; whitecaps,
chefs' hats, prepare
a hot potato-potluck good
on such choppy afternoons. . .

The sky boils and jumps
and does the mambo wambo
and hops and skips around
like a pair of black socks
laundered on the stove.

POÈME NOIR

BRAILLE BALLS
Angry at my wife I drove out to our
Cottage by the lake. Around 1 AM a March shower
Began to fall and when I went out on the porch
To see it I saw a young man lurch
Into the lake with all his clothes on. There
Was nobody else around, the other cottages were
Dark, as was mine. He kept walking straight out
And soon the water was over his head. I shout-
Ed but he obviously didn't hear. He was trying
To drown himself! So I swam out and grabbed him. Sighing,
I resuscitated him. He lay on our bed
Smiling. Thanks a lot but no thanks, he said.
Then he convinced me that no matter what I did
He was going to commit suicide.
I had an idea: Does it make any difference how
You do it? I asked him. No, he replied,
What do you mean. Well, what about the electric

I WANT MY FRIENDS IN WOODY LOTS,
WITH FRENCH TOAST UP THEIR NOSTRILS
Chair? Would you care if it was that? No,
He said. Well I'll send ten thousand dollars
To anyone you cite, if you'll kill my wife and
Go to the electric chair for it. Yes,
He said, I'll pretend to be a burglar, kill her, then get
Caught. Send the ten grand to N, who rejected me. She'll
Feel sorrier then when I'm dead. He grinned. I
Said, Great. The next night I slipped
My wife 2 sleeping-pills then drove to my brother's
To try to establish an alibi but he got drunk,

Passed out so that was no go—damn.
When I got home I went right to my wife's room where
I found her snoring. What the hell, I said. Then
The phone rang. It was my brother,
He said someone had murdered our father. Father!
I said. A hectic day followed. Police, the tax
Lawyers, not to mention, my worthless alibi.
Finally that night I sat waiting for the guy

OCTOBER
Who was to murder my wife. The phone rang. My
Brother had been killed! I was chief suspect
Since I inherited the family millions. Wake up, wake up,
I shook my wife, but the 3 sleeping-pills etcetera.
The police followed me all the next day
But I slipped them. They didn't know I was hitting all the
    joints
To try and find that young drown man. We
Had a few things to discuss: That night
Down by the deserted docks we fought.
I was slugged into the river and I drowned.
No-one ever saw him. When they found
My body the coroner ruled suicide over remorse at my terrible
    crimes.
He had done the murders but I got the blame.
My wife got all the money, and married him.

OCTOBER

The leaves fall, but not far enough for me,
so I take one up to the top of my favorite highrise,
the one whose TV-transmitters watch farmers.
Out over the roof-edge I drop it, but my eye
swerves to the hemline of a nearby tourist.
I wonder if anyone will prefer it. The wind
is certain to vacillate its journey;
a vacillation is a vagueness with intent,
and my leaf is light. —And has her camera
caught me in the act, prolonging it even further—
Her blouse blows but now I notice most how
she caresses the camera, fondly, a personal
touch placed on what is after all a mere
automaton winking a robot eye. . .hmm, are mechanisms,
like, say, money, or credit-cards, are they
harder to put one's traits on than a flower
for instance, or an ear of corn. . .For example
I know someone who has a five-dollar-bill
taped up on her wall with the name "Frank
Sinatra" scribbled across it, an autograph,
according to her, but is writing (or forging)
your name on money or on a machine,—?!
does a signature make it more human, natural,
leafier somehow. . .hell, money is not a good
example, it's not mechanic, I'm sorry. Damn.
Back on the track: the leaf falls, the farmers
farm and the tourist films till her camera's
involuntary functions are exhausted. . .
we head back down. The elevator control-panel blinks
like a flightdeck, or Star Trek or something,

then I notice buttons on her skirtfront—
I punch all the buttons on my shirtfront,
not knowing which direction that will get me,
yet suspecting that it too will not be far enough.

CRASH COURSE

1.
I strap a TV monitor on my chest
so that all who approach me can see themselves
and respond appropriately.

2.
The one in the armchair shooting up
is 19, loads of fun, a goodguy. Her boyfriend
is at the picture-window, begins his monologue.

Whatever they're discussing,
it comes with a lot of windmilly arm gestures:
a kind of Hindu deity; or maybe a whirlpool deity.

3.
The eyelids are not as fast as
a compactor in a factory.
Now something flat, something hard
gets stamped out—it gleams.

PROBLEM

My life has been attributed to someone else. Defeats, victories,
   loves, hates,
all categorized with that person's name.

I belong whether I like it to the School of
the Genre of
the Age of that so and so.

All my acts bear as an adverb their name with an esque on
   the end:
I cross my legs ————————esquely;
my words are all ————————esque—that's right,
yes, I don't even know whose
name I'm speaking of nor why everything I do's described
with that appellation, that trademark.

It might be worse if I did know
I might be tempted to go look up
her or him
and bluster, *Now let's get this straight*
or *What's going on here*

That's just wish. In real life I'd get the address wrong, mistake
   their nextdoor neighbor for them:
Boy, this is a nice apartment.

Nor would it be any kind of consolation whatsoever
if I did confront them and find out
that THEY suffer the same displacement only
under the name of someone in the near town which
if that was so would imply or infer that similarly, somewhere,
there's someone
who has my name stuck on all their efforts. . .

No, I can't see any answer to this problem—
not marxist, nor freudian, kafkaesque, rilkean, knottic,
—because any solution,
any amelioration just ends up being added on to the front end
    of the adjectives
which already encrust the thing, and that just adds to, adds
    to. . .

—Though if it's a choice of spinning out vapid tautologies
or,
Hi/Nice to meet you/I've heard a lot about, I'd
rather just credit this poem to someone else, forget the
    schmear-thing, disappear, move to the far town, entertain
    aliases, take Senile Ed classes in the art of fingerprint
    arrangement, scrub raw the whole per se of identity,
    destiny, ancestor-bashing, make a citizen's arrest of my
    mirror for indecent exposure, but never, nowhere, nohow

will I do penance, beg forgiveness for
any of my failures ascribed to you or
your successes circa me—.

GUILTY CREATURES AT PLAY

Theme-gun open on my lap I am trying
to summon the only vice
best practiced in public
so I can ram it up the ditto virtue in private
A flyspeck feast, a ficcione if you will
for minor depthgaze officials
or folklorists who kneel to ask
"Yes, but is it Grade-A gutbucket?"

Memory is just an echo that's
believed its ears once too often
you whisper to Alias the Big Diaper
"Like a cash-register I get my biggest thrill banging zeroes"
It was that kind of day
The kind that goes through you
like a skewer but is okay as long
as there's someone beside you
waiting ready to lick the skewer
when it emerges from you

You know those hollows, those sockets
collarbones make at the base of your neck?
well today I wanted silver dollars placed in mine
I don't ask for much, you replied
But first, cut the bait off your eyelashes will you

I was at my desk
it was covered with symbols of irritation
the ballpointpens in particular
they had the look of accusatory linebreaks

I tried to phone you but I remembered the expression on my
    face
so I stopped
It was nothing in particular
Probably it was one of those faces we made
while being born
one of those pouts, gnarls, scowls, smiles, pursings
I can't remember which

They didn't have super-8 back then
Fassbinder could do it, you say reaching
for another ilk-self to wipe with
What about clones armed with finger-groins I point out
Yeah Okay But isn't that a little like
trying to establish or abolish a fad (say, Apologetic Chic)
    or, no,
no, it's an insincere murder-ballad
just squatting itself down there in the inner provincial
that foci loci place
where you are marked for goodbye as others for hello
Besides, how does one say Hello
in SOS-language?

Other times we were struck by the will to tie
a disco to a duck's foot
or watch a suit-of-armor chew its fingernails
while we assumed the fetal position
with a beachball
My womb-envy was furious
I stabbed a straw down through my bellybutton I sipped

Hello you said, Information?
Hi. No I don't want a number I just wanted to tell you
that the deserter from our graveyard
should be nearing your graveyard any second
Are you still trying to get that guy I muttered
he's nothing but an aftershave shaman

I was probably jealous
it was like that painting that time
where the artist had a whole bunch of frames
stuck onto the original frame
so you had to look down a tunnel of these frames
to see the painting
I felt a bit intimidated slighted humiliated
like when I pretend not to recognize
the confectioner of my toenails
as we pass on the street
and on top of that by the time my gaze had got to the end
of that tunnel it was too late somehow
to see the painting
It was as if my forearms and wrists
kept trying to grasp at to catch hold of
my hands but can't they can't reach that far
And then
there's that slang phrase I used to use
This scene, pause for effect, sucks the big one

Remember that day we took my loveletters
to you and had them pulped and papier-mached and
made into a paperweight with which to hold
your other loveletters down safe from the hoo-ha wind
But on the other hand
that day also looked like some of my poems
usually the ones where ersatz europeanisms
bronc to shake off their quotemark yokes
or whine to be de-italicized

But when we looked back at our footprints
in that mud
they had indeed been sheeted with stained-glass
I tried to imagine someone really sitting
at an assemblyline
plucking thorns off plastic roses
but it was pointless

but it
but it was my attempt to atone for harboring "transmarine
   tastes"
(as the Assimilationist Lowell put it)
my apology for
becoming a Neocolonialist

I had a wen on my forehead
to which I traveled occasionally
On the way back one day something happened
Or maybe it was just something covered with happen-sauce
An invitation to the White House? unh—an
expurgated handshake flies up and down the
receptionline
I knew it was all and au courant because I had written a book
   just like it
A book consisting of one word
printed over and over again
The word was "attentionspan"
which is my favorite word
because I can never finish
reading it all the way through

Later of us we were trying to balance mirrors
atop our umbilical-cords
but they kept falling off
in the air
And you kept saying "Well look, he's a stickler for me
and you aren't"
I smiled at the word, it made me a placard for a while

You tie me to a chair
and give alms to the garbage-bag
Later of me I think it's a novelist who wrote
that you alone know how to trace
the successive identities of a scar
through the welcome-mat

nailed across my mirror
Then another day I was busy
leaning between 2 pillars of sunglasses
or correcting misprints in the word "I"
when our conceits merged like a proofreader's eyes
Suddenly I understood
your need to die flipping a cardex
for the name of the one who loved you to a lapse, glorious

"Of course the expedition to determine the inroads
of rheumatism upon the Sphinx is a front,"
you used to say, "but for what?
What!?—when For Sale signed faces thicken
every church jettisoned from our countdown's years?!"
Geopolitics made you adamant
You often added:
"And yet their incomparable Alamo will
be crushed, the Bastille fall, fade backwater-wards, be
just a glacier's pitstop, scraped, lost"

I don't know about yours
but my parachute has a smudge on it
so I think I'll jump pure
I promised

IV

UNTOWARD SITES

THE MISUNDERSTANDING

I'm charmed yet chagrined by this misunderstanding
As when, after a riot my city's smashed-in stores appear all
Boarded up, billboarded over, with ads for wind-insurance.
Similarly, swimmingly, I miss the point. You too?

And my misunderstanding doesn't stop there, it grows—soon
I can't see why that sudden influx of fugitives,
All the world's escapees, rubbing themselves lasciviously against
    the Berlin Wall.
They stick like placards to it. Like napalm. Like ads for—

And me, I haven't even bought my biodegradable genitalia yet!
No. I was born slow, but picking up speed I run through
Our burnt-out streets, screaming, refusing to buy a house.
Finally, exasperated, the misunderstanding overtakes me,
    snatches up

Handcuffs. So now here I am, found with all you others
Impatiently craning, in this line that rumors out of sight up
    ahead somewhere,
Clutching our cash eager to purchase whatever it is, nervous
As if bombs were about to practice land-reform upon our
    bodies,

Redistribution of eyes, toes, arms, here we stand. Then, some
    new Age starts.

DEPRESSIONISM

Without any necessity to name it or anything,
I remember this bombcrater before it held a garden.
Once I saw children kneel down there to pray for pardon
At an altar on which a little toll-money rolled laughing.

Swift suedes of evening, night's purple peltdown.
I don't have to invoke the past; it's not required.
I'll just settle here stolid like a stopsign repeating
The word I stand for—sit and let my tired feet hang

Over the lip of this pit-deep garden whose intricate
Vines query up at me. Quiet from the town I can hear
Orphans rattling the gravel on their plates and or

Other faux pas I'm under no order to enumerate,—
Jet-lag of angels, a snake, faintings on summer pavements.
This bombfall failed in its intent: having none, I won't.

THE QUESTION

Far off, demimordial, I hear an epitaph of ears, someone
Collides with a stopwatch, innocent mincemeats rise steaming
   and
Sporadic laughter, cardoors going slammed. Then static-ier
   voices,
Through blood jettisoned by mimes, statues reminisce, reveal
   how
They subsist on glimpsed nubility, personal-touches in crowds
   who
Traipse past. In rooms where you heard the sound of a tear-
   drop
Striking the bloodhound surface of perfume which sat in a
Washbasin, chipped fake porcelain, who poured it in that? in
Those rooms (where you were so strangely audient!) others,
   like
Me, are listening. Outside, in the city, the minstrelshow
Pollution (which paints us all in "blackface") continues, corny
And racist, sexist, lampoonist. . .humanist? Ashes watered
By hell, kisses skimmed from doveflight, cream from silk, what-
Ever rises, curdled, from depths as fraught with else as these,
Far off. . .Yet I would encourage your traits your tricks indi-
   vidual
Of speech, you crowds who gape on as those rooms all rush
   toward
One room whose doors part now like a mouth pried in cry
Silently, stifled by its openness. Will my voice receive me,
Will my cries still have me? will not be the question there.

LOURDES

There are miracles that nobody survives
No one comes screaming of where what when
And these are the only true miracles
Since we never hear tell about them—

Since we never hear tell about them
It increases their chance of being common
Everyday events without witness without
Us even—how absently close we brush

Teeth sneeze cook supper mail postcards
In contrast official miracles take a far
Off locale some backwater—or podunk
Which although unverifiable is visitable

Not pop the map but part the pilgrim's
Lips it springs up hospitals hot dog
Stands pour in testosteroniacs pimple
Victims but most of all cripples—their

Limbs misled and skewed and crisscross
Like—roadsigns that point everywhere
On a signpost bent over a weedy crossroads
In the boondocks of a forgotten place

VACANCIES, OCCUPANCIES

FOR JANE SHORE

1.
I want to be an all fours thing.
Worse: dozered, razed
past hands and knees: hail any
horizon as apogee.

2.
A sniper lies on all
the roofs. Years
pass rude. Resigned their aims;
voluble ivy twines
the triggerfinger.

3.
Hearing something familiar,
I stepped to the window.
Rain slapped on the sill.
An ocean presenting its birth
certificate, demanding a passport. Later
the sky came through in places,
but pale, residual, as blueprints are
the day their site's topped off—

4.
The one face I will never find between my teeth
continues to quote me.

Don't think, it sneers,
that just because I deny myself in your presence
I do so in mine.

5.
The eyes, built on a ruins which is
the skull, rise.

THE COMMUTER'S DREAM

Every morning an afterdinner-mint
dissolves around us.   In it, cars touch,

like tiny hands at a football huddle—
headlights.   Rushhour pushes through mist

or dark its stubborn, pre-peekaboo path;
a worm fed into a pencil-sharpener.

READING THE GAPS

At the Museum I go lost down a wrong corridor
and find myself through a wrong door alone
inside the Museum's bombshelter, I know
it's the bombshelter because there's a green
sign that says so and the paintings, the
paintings they have hung on display here,
confirm it—Oh Archilochos! to quote one
of your lesser surviving fragments the
fishnets lie in shadow beneath the wall but
there is no shadow beneath this wall and
your fishnets, stretched, are these paintings I
can't for life see why I can't describe—maybe
they're too much like a mirror, a mirror
that's been squeezed into an icicle dripping
its faces on me—this discountenanced chill
descends I know from 3 thousand years of
megadeaths squeezed rammed into the nucleus
of this decision moment of Break Glass In
Case Of Emergency, fire-hose, ax, no, I can't
proffer these in violence against those
paintings they portray my face my fate their
paint drips from that blasted-down wall where
drying fishnets spread a shade a shield for this
most ancient warrior and forelast poet—

Later, in the restaurant as usual I dip the
wine-list into a glass of water and voila it's
chablis because of course miracles are
common now whereas the latter hope of living
to read tomorrow today's lacunae isn't.

SUDDEN DEPARTURE

A sudden raisinstorm broke
Raisins falling everywhere pellmell.
The occasion uniqued my head, I thought
If this can happen raisins raining
Upon persons paining why I can leave anytime
Without feeling shame.

But, all the same,
Before taking off some vestigial guilt or other
Made me at least get up
Before some public gathering or other
A departing oration:

Druthers, I am going now.
Druthers, I tried to love you
Though you always made me choose
Between you, you, and you. Oh my druthers,

Goodbye. I have my reasons.

Did he say RAISINS?
No: reasons.
Oh; I just wondered,
What with the weather and all.

FEEDING THE SUN

One day we notice that the sun
needs feeding. Immediately
a crash program begins: we fill rockets
with wheat, smoke-rings, razorblades, then,
after long aiming
—they're off. Hulls specially alloyed
so as not to melt before the stuff
gets delivered we pour cattle rivers windmills,
aborigines etcet into the sun which
however, grows stubbornly
smaller, paler. Finally
of course we run out of things to feed the thing,
start shipping ourselves. By now
all the planets-moons-asteroids and
so on have been shoveled in though they're
not doing much good it's
still looking pretty weak, heck, nothing helps!
Now the last few of us left lift off.
The trip seems forever but then, touchdown.
Just before entering we wonder,
will we be enough. There's
a last-second doubt
in our minds: can we,
can this final sacrifice, our broughten crumb,
satiate
it—will a glutteral belch burst out then at last,—
and will that Big Burp
be seen by far-off telescopes,
interpreted as a nova,
by those other galaxies,

those further stars which have always seemed even more
    starving
than ours?

BILL KNOTT was born in Michigan in 1940. His first book, *The Naomi Poems: Book One: Corpse and Beans,* was published in 1968. It was followed by *Aurealism: A Study; Autonecrophilia: The ——— Poems: Book 2; Nights of Naomi; Love Poems to Myself; Rome in Rome* and *Selected and Collected Poems,* which won the 1978 Elliston Prize. Bill Knott has been poet-in-residence at Columbia College, Thomas Jefferson College, Wright State University and Emerson College in Boston, where he currently teaches. He was awarded a National Endowment for the Arts grant in 1980.